The Blue Collar Guide To Building Wealth

Edmond Alantes

© e.a. 2016

Contents

Introduction 5

What Money Can Buy, and Can't Buy 7

Rules to Wealth 9

   #1- Pay yourself 9

      The 10-70-20 Ratio Plan 10

      Debt Ratio 11

      Living Expense Ratio 12

      Me Payment 12

      Assets and Liabilities 14

   #2- Know Your Expenses 15

   #3- Invest 15

   #4- Be Frugal About Spending 16

   #5- Own You Home 16

   #6- Insure a Future Income 17

   #7- Increase Your Ability to Earn 17

Debt to Income Ratio 19

   Front-End Ratio 19

- Back-End Ratio 20
- Work 21
- Skill, Experience, Opportunity, and Luck 23
- Pay Off Strategy 25
  - The Roll-Over Strategy 25
- Investing 27
  - Stock 27
  - REITS 27
  - Silver Investing 27
    - Troy Ounce 30
    - Junk Silver 30
- Bankruptcy: Extreme Debt Relief 33
- Meeting the Wrong People 35
  - The Sociopath 35
  - Deceptive Landlord Trick 38

Introduction

I wrote this book to be as concise as possible; short and to the point. I could have easily made this book close to 400 pages and charged close to $30 for it. But I want you to *save* money not spend it. I want this information to be affordable and accessible to the people who need it the most. Wealth building is simple, but it takes dedication. There are no secrets to wealth building, and there is no reason to make complicate things. All that's needed to build wealth is the dedication to follow a few simple rules. Wealth will not happen overnight, but you will, in time, build a comfortable wealth as long as you follow these rules. In fact, if you adhere to the basic rules you will notice a difference in your financial comfort within three months! Of course you won't be "wealthy" in three months, but you will feel and realize the potential of the 10-70-30 system. I can't promise you a million dollars, but I can promise you comfortable wealth.

Edmond Alantes

What Money Can Buy, and Can't Buy

What would you do if you were wealthy?

- ✓ Go on vacation?
- ✓ Buy a mansion?
- ✓ Buy and expensive car?

If you answered YES to any of these questions, that's why you're not wealthy! Do wealthy people buy these things, yes, and no. It depends on how wealthy a person is. Very wealthy people can afford these things. They have very high paying jobs, or own very productive businesses. Purchasing a car or a home is more than just being able to afford the purchase price; it's being able to maintain the purchase as well. You will have maintenance cost, insurance, taxes, heat, air conditioning, etc. In *The Millionaire Next Door* by T.J. Stanley and W.D. Danko, they were surprised to realize that the majority of the millionaires interviewed for the book did not purchase their cars brand new; they purchased second hand cars, usually two or three years old. They all expressed that it didn't make monetary sense to buy something that depreciates after you drive it off the lot.

Money will not by financial freedom if you use that money to put yourself further in debt. Saving and investing will earn you financial freedom. Money does not buy love, happiness, or friendship either. How many miserable rich people do you hear about? And then there are friends that always seem to show up when you're buying the next round. I heard a saying about happiness that goes; Happiness is not finding the right person, it's being the right person.

Rules to Wealth

#1- Pay yourself

The first and most important rule is that 10% of the money you earn in yours to keep. "But", you might ask, "All my money is already mine, is it not?" No it isn't, you have bills, debt obligations, kids and whatever else you need to live. People spend their life paying their bills without ever paying themselves. The road to wealth is paying yourself first, before you pay anyone else. You will not even miss 10% of your money, and if you can put away more that's even better. If you choose to pay yourself at least 10% of your money now and every payday from this point on or not, in ten years you'll be glad you did, or you'll wish you had!

There are two things I will require you to do, this is to open two separate savings accounts. One is a savings account, if you don't already have one, which is connected to your checking account. This is your Emergency Savings that is used for unforeseen events like auto repairs and the like. The next savings account, possibly in a different bank or Credit Union is your Me

Account. This is used to deposit your Me Payments. The money you put into your savings for your Me Payment stays there. It is only to be used for further investing. Not for buying a new motorcycle or Skeet gun.

I would also suggest keeping a notebook with each page dedicated to your monthly income and expenditures. Keeping track of your finances will help you build a healthy plan and good financial habits. And it will make it easier for you when the time comes to review and revise your financial plan.

The 10-70-20 Ratio Plan

The 10-70-20 Ratio is where all your money should be going. 10% goes to savings; this is your Me Payment. 70% goes for Living Expense, and 20% toward Debt. This covers 100% of your earnings. That's it; there is no more, if you add to one you have to take from another.

The 10-70-20 Finance Plan

10 - 70 - 20

Me Payment	Living Expense	Debt
Savings Deposit	Housing Expense	Credit Cards
	(incl. Mortgage)	Auto Payment
	Food	2nd Mortgage
	Recreation	
	Clothing	

This diagram is in no way complete, but it shows a good idea of how earnings are allocated.

Debt Ratio

According to the powers-that-be your debt payments should not exceed 35%. But this would turn the ratio to 10-55-35 or even worse 0-65-35. The optimal debt ratio is 20%, this will give you the most freedom to enjoy life and the things around you. If your debt payments are over 35% you have to bring it down by paying off some of your creditors. This should be a priority.

Your Debt Ratio includes all your liabilities except your first mortgage. It would also include alimony payments and child support if you have these obligations.

Living Expense Ratio

The optimal Living Expense is 70% of your earnings. This includes your housing expense, insurance payments, food, heating oil, recreation expense, and any other expense you use to live and enjoy your life.

You will also make deposits into your Emergency Savings as part of your living expense. In this account you can allocate a small portion of your earnings for emergencies. Many people too often resort to credit cards when an unexpected auto or home repair comes up. If you can knock out one of your credit card debts and allocate the payment you were making to that card to this "emergency" account, you will have a small savings to help you when an unforeseen event occurs.

Me Payment

The Me Payment is the backbone of this system and the key to your wealth. At least 10% of your earnings should be allocated to yourself, this is rule #1. Rule #2 is not to touch this money unless it's an investment that will make more money. The money made from this investment should be put back into the Me account. Rule #3 is you need a steady cash flow; you have to work hard to achieve wealth. Never think of your work as a burden, think of it as the key to your wealth and happiness. Rule #4: Don't live above your means. The amount of your income should have no bearing on your wealth. Wealth is relative to what you earn and how much you spend. Sure a man who has greater earnings will be able to buy more expensive things, but if he is living outside his means he is spending more than he should and is putting himself in debt. In this respect it is possible that a "poorer" man can have more wealth than a "richer" man. Rule #5, and just as important as rule #1, is to be humble and treat people with respect. You will have greater luck and open the doors to more opportunity if you treat the people you meet along the way with respect. You will encounter some people who are disrespectful and treat people indifferent. Don't let them influence you, stay humble, their actions will have a negative effect on them sooner or later.

Assets and Liabilities

Assets and Liabilities are different than Income and Expense. Your Income is the money you earn; Expense is the money you spend. An Asset is a thing that earns you money, and a Liability is what costs you money. Your job is an asset; your electric bill is a liability. A new car is a liability; the money you spend on it is your expense. Your home is actually a liability as well as an investment as it is costing you monthly payments. Your home is not listed under your Debt Ratio because no matter what, you have to spend money to live somewhere whether that expenditure is rent or mortgage.

When you get in over your head with debt it is called a **deficit**, which is when your liabilities exceed your assets.

A raise, and investment, or any other asset that increases you income should not be used to make more purchases. It should be made to payoff existing debt and applied to your savings. For example, an increase of $100 per week: $10 should go to your Me Account, $70 to living, and $20 to debt. Or if your bills are settled it would be nice to add the majority of your increase to your Me Account. When any change in asset or liability occurs you should review and rework your 10-70-20 plan.

#2- Know Your Expenses

Make a list of all your expenses and how much they cost. Then create a monthly payment system to pay your bills on time. With a good system you should be able to pay your bills at the correct amount even if you didn't receive your monthly statement. Keep active with your budget, and revise it accordingly if any payments change. Factor in necessities and things you enjoy, but don't go overboard on enjoyment!

#3- Invest

I'll get into investments later on but for now know that your Me Payments should be used to create more wealth. When looking into investment opportunities make sure you talk with professionals in the field, and know the risks involved. If you hear about an investment that has no negative aspects and can't fail, count on it failing! Avoid money making schemes; creating wealth is like the turtle in the race, slow and steady!

#4- Be Frugal About Spending

Don't be in a rush to see every new film that comes out in the movie theatre. If you need something, shop around for the best price. And by the same token don't buy the cheapest item you can find, you usually get what you pay for and will spend more money in the long run.

#5- Own You Home

If you don't already own a home, make that a priority. It doesn't have to be waterfront property with its own boating dock. There are Condos, the Small Home movement, log cabins and House Boats to name a few options. When you do purchase a home, make sure you can afford the taxes. The best option is to have your property taxes included in your monthly payments.

#6- Insure a Future Income

We can't work forever, though some of us would like to! Some people buy properties to rent for an income, creative works can produce royalties, open a small business, the list of ides can go on.

Many people turn their hobbies into lucrative businesses. Whatever your hobby or favorite pastime is there's a good chance you can turn it into a viable income.

#7- Increase Your Ability to Earn

This means to educate yourself in financial and business knowledge. Read books on sales, marketing, entrepreneurship, business management. There are many books by regular people, just like us, who have Cinderella stories; they went from rags to riches. Read their stories and get inspired, especially if they used the same pastime or hobby that you enjoy and created a business out of it. Even if not, these stories are very inspiring and educational.

Debt to Income Ratio

Front-End Ratio

The front-end ratio is what mortgage lenders use to indicate how much of a portion of your income is used to make your mortgage payments. You can use the front-end ratio to determine what your maximum housing expense should be, whether you rent or pay mortgage. The front-end ratio should be about 30% of your earnings, but no more than 40%. In the 10-70-20 Finance Plan your front-end ratio is part of your 70% living ratio. A 30% front-end ratio would leave 40% of your earnings for other living expenses; if it is at 40% you have 30% for other living expenses. Any front-end ratio over 40% you are starting to live above your means and you'll have less money to do your laundry, go to a movie, buy a book, and even eat.

Front-End Ratio

Maximum Housing Expense Ratio

Annual salary X .30 / 12

Multiply your annual salary by .30 (30%), divide the result by 12 (12 monthly payments).

Back-End Ratio

The back-end ratio is also known as the debt-to-income ratio. This ratio indicates what portion your earnings go toward paying debts. The optimal ratio is 20%, but should never exceed 35%.

Back-End Ratio

Debt-To-Income Ratio

Annual salary X .20 / 12

Multiply your annual salary by .20 (20%), divide the result by 12. This will give you the maximum amount of your earnings that should be allocated to debt.

Work

The principle of hard work is that it is worth of reward. There are only a 4 principles to follow when it comes to work; be humble, be reliable, be fair, and always do the right thing. If it feels wrong, it is wrong; people always know when they're doing something wrong.

If you are college educated, or plan to go to college, remember this does not mean you do not have to work hard. On the contrary, you have to work even harder as your education makes you a professional in your field and you are expected to be a positive example to others. In Viking History the kings themselves would have a turn at rowing the ship! Hard work was considered an honor and no one was above their fair share. Remember to lead by example.

I listed humble first because if you're humble the rest of the principles will come naturally. Being humble is as simple as just making other people feel important. When engaged in conversation always make the other person feel important. Also be a good, sincere listener, all the while encouraging the other person to talk about themselves. Be attentive in the conversation and show sincere appreciation, next to feeling important everyone wants to be appreciated.

Dale Carnegie said; "You can make more friends in two months by becoming interested in other people than you can in two years by trying to get other people interested in you."

When it comes to criticizing people, don't! But, if the situation calls for it and you must offer critical advice, criticize yourself first. Offer an anecdote about yourself in a similar situation, and then make sure your constructive criticism is constructive. It is always better give praise for good actions instead of criticizing for bad actions. Of course poor performance or actions should always be addressed, but there is a respectful way and manner to go about it.

Skill, Experience, Opportunity, and Luck

Skill and Experience bring you to opportunities that others will perceive as luck.

$$Skill = Opportunity = Luck$$

Developing skill will open your way to more opportunities which, in turn, expose you to good luck and fortune. If a young lady studies acting and attends various schools and workshops, meets people of similar interest, takes on free roles in small productions and charity events, then one day is offered the leading role in a major production film, people will say how lucky she was. Was she lucky, partly yes, but she worked hard and studied to put herself in the position for this fortunate luck to find her. If she had stayed home and played games, she would still be home playing games.

"Never mistake Luck for ones effort to place himself in a desirable opportunity. Opportunity and luck travel hand in hand." ~Erick Alayon, Artist/Poet/Photographer

Pay Off Strategy

The Roll-Over Strategy

The Roll-Over Strategy of paying off debt is when you pay extra monthly payments to one debt to pay it off, and then apply the payment from the satisfied debt to the next debt in order to pay that one off early as well. By rolling over payments from satisfied debts and adding them to the next one creates a snowball effect as each payment to the next debt grows larger.

I would suggest starting with credit cards first as these have the most interest. If you have more than one credit card start with the one you owe the least amount of money on. Some advisors will suggest a payoff attempt on the one you owe the most money to, but it will be quicker to satisfy the smaller debt faster and give you a feeling of accomplishment.

To pay off your first debt you might have to give up a luxury item or pastime that you enjoy in order to do this. This temporary setback is worth it in the long run.

I would also advise to fund your Emergency Savings as much as you can. After each satisfied debt allocate a portion of the old payment to your Emergency Savings. This way, if an unforeseen event arises you will have cash to address it instead of using a credit card.

Investing

There are many investment opportunities. Two of the most common are Stock and REITS (Real Estate Investment Trust).

Remember to consult a professional in the type of investment you plan on entering.

Stock

Everyone knows what a stock is but the official definition is that a stock is a form of security in which the owner of the stock actually has ownership in the corporation.

REITS

A REIT is a type of security that people use to invest in real estate. REITS are often traded on major exchanges in the same way a stock is traded. REITs are required by law to maintain a 90% dividend payout, making them a good form of cash flow.

Silver Investing

Investing in Silver is a good way to retain the value of your money. When you see the price of precious metals going up, this is actually the value of the dollar going down. However there are instances when precious metals rise substantially in a price bubble. When this happens you can sell off your silver and when the bubble bursts and the price drops you can repurchase your silver once again and hold a nice, tidy profit. The problem is you never know when a bubble will happen or when it will burst. Before purchasing silver make sure you are in a Buyer's Market first.

25% of your Me Payment is a good portion to allocate to silver. But this decision is yours, if you decide to do it at all.

An example of how silver retains its value is to imagine that you and a friend, in 1990, each decided to save $1000. Your friend puts his money in his sock drawer, and you decide to purchase silver bullion. In 1990 the price of silver averaged around $4.50 per troy ounce. For this example let's say you acquired your silver at this price. At $4.50 per ounce you were able to purchase 222 silver bullion coins. Now let's fast forward to 2010, you and your friend are going on vacation and you each decide to use your savings stash as spending money while you're away. You pick up your friend and he has $1000 dollars in his pocket. You have your silver and stop at a coin dealer to cash them in. Once inside you find out silver is now $20 an ounce! You cash them in and have $4440 in spending money!

The question is did you make money? Theoretically yes, you did. Technically no, you didn't. Well, maybe, but not as much as you think you did anyway. The reason you didn't is because 222 ounces of silver in 1990 would roughly purchase the same value of items in 2010. Silver goes up in price, but not in value, the rise in the price of silver is actually the value of the dollar going down. For example; if you and your friend went on vacation in 1990 and used four silver bullion to buy a sack of oranges, then you returned in 2010 with four pieces of silver, you would still be able to buy roughly the same sack of oranges. In 1990 our theoretical sack of oranges was $18 (don't hold me to this; this is purely for arguments sake. I don't know how much a sack of oranges was in 1990.) But in the year 2001 the same theoretical sack of oranges costs around $80 or so; the same value as the four silver coins. The price of oranges went up in accordance with the price of silver. Remember the price of goods and services going up is in reality the value of the dollar going down.

Troy Ounce

A troy ounce is used to measure precious metals. A troy ounce is 31.1 grams. A troy ounce is slightly heavier than a regular ounce which is 28.35 grams (1.097 oz.).

Junk Silver

Junk Silver are regular coins in the denominations of dollars, half dollars quarters, and dimes minted in 1964 and older. They contain 90% silver and 10% copper (Except the 1965-1970 Half Dollar and the 1971-1976 Eisenhower Dollar which contain (40% silver). The melt value of these coins takes both the silver and copper into consideration. The following is a list of America Silver Coins:

- 1892-1916 Barber Dime
- 1916-1945 Mercury Dime

- 1946-1964 Roosevelt Dime
- 1892-1916 Barber Quarter
- 1916-1930 Standing Liberty Quarter
- 1932-1964 Washington Quarter
- 1892-1915 Barber Half Dollar
- 1916-1947 Walking Liberty Half Dollar
- 1948-1963 Franklin Half Dollar
- 1964 Kennedy Half Dollar
- 1965-1970 Half Dollar (40% silver)
- 1878-1921 Morgan Dollar
- 1921-1935 Peace Dollar
- 1971-1976 Eisenhower Dollar (40% silver)

Weight of American Silver Coins:

- Dime- 2.5 grams
- Half Dollar- 12.5 grams
- Half Dollar 40%- 11.5 grams
- Dollar- 26.73 grams
- Dollar 40%- 24.59 grams

To determine the silver value of these coins you have to multiply the metal price by .0321507466 to convert it into grams. This result is multiplied by the weight of the coin, this result is then multiplied by .90, which is the percentage of silver (If you were trying to determine the value of a 40% coin you would then multiply by .40).

Bankruptcy: Extreme Debt Relief

Bankruptcy is an option of debt relief when all other options fail. For example if you lose your job and are now working at a lower salary, or if you, like many people, just got in over your head with credit card debt. Bankruptcy can also save your home from foreclosure. The best thing to do if you are considering bankruptcy is to talk to a professional bankruptcy attorney. I say professional because there are many unscrupulous lawyers out there. Stay away from the ones that offer bankruptcy at a very low rate, they don't care about you, all they want is your money and their law firm is run like a busy meat market.

There are six types of bankruptcy; they are Chapter 7, 9, 11, 12, 13, and 15. Personal bankruptcies are usually Chapter 7 and Chapter 13, which type you can file is determined by your income. Chapter 7 is the most common of the two. Basically the only debts that you cannot alleviate are student loans, child support, certain tax debt, and criminal fines; most other debts are discharged. There are circumstances where your home is protected under Chapter 7, you must consult a professional.

In a Chapter 13 bankruptcy you can retain possession of all of your assets, this includes your home. However in a Chapter 13 your lawyer will submit a payment plan to the trustee in which you have 3 to 5 years to pay all your debts. Depending on how much you owe will determine the amount and the time allotted to pay it off. Chapter 13 payments can put you on a very strict budget for up to five years as the majority of your disposable income will be going to paying off your debt. If your home is in foreclosure the money you owe the bank will be included in your monthly Chapter 13 payments and under federal law the bank cannot foreclose on your property.

Meeting the Wrong People

Most people you encounter on your journey through life will be honest, hardworking people. If you encounter too many people who are not, you're hanging out with the wrong crowd. When you associate with good, productive people, good fortune will find you. When you associate with negative and manipulative people you will become stagnant and possibly lose everything you worked hard for.

Avoid negative people like the plague; these are people who always point out the bad side of everything. No matter who you associate with and no matter how much you try to avoid negative, deceptive people, you will still encounter them from time to time. They're at your work, in the gym, and they're even friends of friends you'll meet at social gatherings.

The Sociopath

Avoid people who are manipulative, who lie, who are shallow, show contempt, and lack remorse for anything they do wrong. These are dangerous people, and upon meeting them don't be rude; just excuse yourself somehow if you're able. At work this might be difficult, but try to avoid these people as best you can without causing animosity. Most of these people are Sociopaths, 1 in 25 people are said to exhibit sociopathic behavior, the more you know and understand about this behavior, the easier it is for you to avoid. A sociopath is a person who has Antisocial Personality Disorder. They have no regard for other people's feelings; they lack remorse and shame, they display a very manipulative behavior, are very egocentric, and have the ability to lie and manipulate in order to achieve their goals to the point of it being an art form.

These people can and will stand in the way of you achieving your goals if given the opportunity, and should be avoided. The main thing is you don't want to get one of these people on your bad side as they will go out of their way to hurt you. To recognize these people look for the following behavior characteristics:

Sociopaths can be very charming people on the outside, but are very manipulative and domineering. To them people are to be used in order for them to achieve their goals, once their goal is reached they are done with you and move on to the next victim.

The sociopath enjoys humiliating people, especially in public or around friends. After doing so they will show no remorse, empathy, or sympathy. They also have no shame or guilt, and can even show contempt for other people's feelings. To them people are only targets of opportunity. They have a sense of entitlement. If you have something they want you have to share it with them, or give it to them outright or they will attempt to make you feel guilty for not surrendering your property. They are not concerned about ruining other people's lives and dreams and show indifference to the devastation they cause. They will never accept blame, and will go as far to blames others for their own destructive actions!

They are very shallow people with an incapacity for love. When a sociopath does show love it is usually fake and serves an ulterior motive. Some of these people do have families and love their family. But when it comes to outsiders, everyone serves a purpose. They have no regard of the negative impact their actions have on others.

They are pathological liars. They will lie to get what they want, to get pity, and will even lie about things that are meaningless. Many sociopaths are so good at lying they are even able to pass a lie detector test!

Avoid people showing these traits, even negative people who are not as extremely dangerous as the sociopath can still have a negative effect on your life.

Deceptive Landlord Trick

This is a very underhanded trick used by very unscrupulous Landlords when they collect rent from unsuspecting tenants. Most people that do this are full aware of what they're doing.

Let's say for example that as a tenant you pay $1000 a month rent. Your Landlord offers to do you a favor and collect $250 on a weekly basis to "make things easier." It sounds innocent enough, right? Wrong! The Landlord is basing your monthly payment on a four week month. The problem with this is that there are 13 four week months in a year! So you are paying him one extra month every year. I'll show you the math; there are 52 weeks in a year, divide 52 by 4 and the result is 13! A four week month is only 28 days; the only month that is 28 days long is February. Every other month is longer than four weeks by a few days. By doing you a "favor" the Landlord is stealing one extra monthly payment per year, any Judge in a Court of Law will know this.

To resolve an issue like this either make regular monthly payments or calculate what your real weekly payment should be. To figure this, simply multiply your monthly payment x 12 (months in a year), then divide the result by 52 (weeks in a year). This result is what your actual weekly payment should be. The weekly payment for $1000 monthly rent would be $230.77, and at the end of a year he would still owe you four cents!

Calculate Monthly Payments to Weekly

Monthly payment X 12 / 52

Of course if you're paying off a set debt, for example $1200 with monthly payments of $100 a month, it would take one year to satisfy this debt. Now if you paid your debtor $25 dollars a week you would pay the debt off in approximately 11 months. 48 weeks to be exact, as opposed to a full year of 52 weeks.

notes